······· Let's Celebrate Latino Holidays ·······

CHRISTMAS

······· Sadie Silva ·······

Please visit our website, www.enslow.com. For a free color catalog of all our high-quality books, call toll free 1-800-398-2504 or fax 1-877-980-4454.

Library of Congress Cataloging-in-Publication Data
Names: Silva, Sadie, author.
Title: Christmas / Sadie Silva.
Description: New York : Enslow Publishing, [2023] | Series: Let's Celebrate Latino Holidays | Includes index.
Identifiers: LCCN 2021037514 (print) | LCCN 2021037515 (ebook) | ISBN 9781978527201 (library binding) | ISBN 9781978527188 (paperback) | ISBN 9781978527195 (set) | ISBN 9781978527218 (ebook)
Subjects: LCSH: Christmas–Latin America–Juvenile literature. | Christmas–United States–Juvenile literature. | Hispanic Americans–Social life and customs. | Posadas (Social custom)–Juvenile literature. | Latin America–Social life and customs.
Classification: LCC GT4987.155 .S55 2023 (print) | LCC GT4987.155 (ebook) | DDC 394.2663098–dc23
LC record available at https://lccn.loc.gov/2021037514
LC ebook record available at https://lccn.loc.gov/2021037515

First Edition

Portions of this work were originally authored by Marisa Orgullo and published as *Celebrating Christmas!*. All new material this edition authored by Sadie Silva.

Published in 2023 by
Enslow Publishing
29 E. 21st Street
New York, NY 10010

Copyright © 2023 Enslow Publishing

Designer: Katelyn Reynolds
Interior Layout: Rachel Rising
Editor: Caitie McAneney

Photo credits: Cover, Creativa Images/Shutterstock.com; Cover, pp. 1-4, 6, 8, 10, 12, 14, 16, 18, 20, 22-24 (background) Cienpies Design/Shutterstock.com; Cover, pp. 1, 3, 23, 24 (text box) scoutori/Shutterstock.com; Cover, pp. 1, 3, 23, 24 (text) Cienpies Design/Shutterstock.com; p. 5 Amy Corti/Shutterstock.com; p. 7 Joseph Sorrentino/Shutterstock.com; p. 9 Fer Gregory/Shutterstock.com; p. 11 Mauro Rodrigues/Shutterstock.com; p. 13 Edaccor/Shutterstock.com; p. 15 Daniel B4nda/Shutterstock.com; p. 17 antoniodiaz/Shutterstock.com; p. 19 Rawpixel.com/Shutterstock.com; p. 21 Marcos Castillo/Shutterstock.com; p. 22 Paragorn Dangsombroon/Shutterstock.com.

All rights reserved. No part of this book may be reproduced in any form without permission in writing from the publisher, except by a reviewer.

Printed in the United States of America

Some of the images in this book illustrate individuals who are models. The depictions do not imply actual situations or events.

CPSIA compliance information: Batch #CSENS23: For further information contact Enslow Publishing, New York, New York, at 1-800-398-2504.

Find us on

CONTENTS

La Navidad 4
Las Posadas 6
Christmas Customs 10
Gifts of the Three Wise Men 16
Glossary 23
For More Information 24
Index 24

Words in the glossary appear in **bold** type the first time they are used in the text.

La Navidad

La Navidad (nah-vee-THAHD) is a special time for Latin Americans and **Latino** people in the United States. It's the Christmas season! People prepare for Christmas, which is December 25th. Christmas **celebrates** the birth of Jesus Christ. People spend time with their families and friends. They take part in Christmas **traditions**.

This big Christmas tree sits in front of a large church in Arequipa, Peru.

Las Posadas

Las Posadas (poh-SAH-thahs) is a nine-day celebration that begins December 16 and ends December 24. Las Posadas tells the story of Mary and Joseph, Jesus's parents. **Christians** believe that they had to go from place to place until they found a safe place for Jesus to be born.

These children in Mexico are dressed as Mary and Joseph for Las Posadas.

To honor this story, people pretend to seek shelter in a posada, or **inn**, just like Mary and Joseph. They knock on doors while singing. Each night, an innkeeper finally welcomes them. Inside, a party waits. Everyone sings and eats, and children hit a **piñata**. Many people dress in silver and gold.

People break open piñatas shaped like stars.

Christmas Customs

Some people make or set up a nativity scene, or a *nacimiento* (nah-sih-mee-EN-toh). A *nacimiento* includes a model of a **stable**. People add models of Mary and Joseph inside it. Children place the baby Jesus in his bed on *la Nochebuena* (NOH-chay BWAY-nah), or Christmas Eve.

This nativity scene shows the baby Jesus with his parents inside a stable.

La Nochebuena is an important night in la Navidad. Many families go to church. **Customs** are different from place to place. In Ecuador, people count down the minutes until midnight. In Puerto Rico and the Dominican Republic, people celebrate by singing in the streets. Children open gifts and families share big meals.

Many **Catholics** go to Mass (church service) at midnight on Christmas Eve in Latin America and the United States.

Food is an important part of any celebration! Many families celebrate Christmas with a feast. Families cook turkey, ham, and special **tamales**. Puerto Ricans eat *pasteles* (pahs-TEL-es), tamales cooked in banana leaves. Mexican children snack on cookies called *biscochitos* (bee-skoh-CHEE-tohs). Panamanians enjoy rice with pineapple.

Tamales are popular foods for celebrations in Latin America, including Christmas.

Gifts of the Three Wise Men

The celebrations are not over on Christmas. People in Latin America also celebrate the Three Wise Men, or *los tres Reyes magos* (TREHS RAY-es MAH-gohs). People believe three kings brought gifts to the baby Jesus. El Día de los Reyes Magos is celebrated January 6. Parades and gifts are common customs on this day.

Children leave out sweets or shoes at night for the Wise Men. In the morning, they wake up to gifts.

17

Children in Puerto Rico have a special custom for Día de los Reyes Magos. They place boxes of grass under their beds on the night of January 5. They believe that this grass is for the Three Wise Men's camels to eat. Then they wake up to presents!

The Three Wise Men are often pictured on camels.

People from Latin America have special treats for Día de los Reyes Magos. *Rosca de reyes* (ROH-skah DAY RAY-es) is the bread of kings. This bread is shaped like a ring and filled with dried fruit and nuts. Everyone enjoys a piece with cups of hot chocolate.

Kids sometimes wear crowns as they eat their *rosca de reyes*.

Countries in Latin America all have special traditions for la Navidad! Many Hispanic people take time to celebrate the story of Jesus's birth. Special foods are shared. Special songs are sung. People wish one another Merry Christmas. It's a time to be together and spread joy to all.

GLOSSARY

Catholic A member of the Roman Catholic Church.
celebrate To honor an important moment by doing special things.
Christian A person who believes in the teachings of Jesus Christ.
custom A way of doing things that is usual among the people in a certain group or place.
Latino Someone who lives in Latin America or whose family is from Latin America.
inn A place where travelers can get food and a place to sleep.
piñata A special container filled with candies that people break with a stick.
stable A building in which farm animals are kept and fed.
tamale Cornmeal dough rolled with ground meat or beans and seasoning, wrapped in corn husks, and steamed.
tradition Something that has been done for a long time.

FOR MORE INFORMATION

Books

Depalma, Kate. *Let's Celebrate! Special Days Around the World.* Cambridge, MA: Barefoot Books, 2019.

Heiligman, Deborah. *Celebrate Christmas: With Carols, Presents, and Peace.* Washington, DC, National Geographic Kids, 2016.

Websites

Christmas Traditions in Brazil
www.littlepassports.com/blog/world-holidays/christmas-traditions-brazil/
Check out the world's largest Christmas tree in Brazil.

Mexican Christmas Traditions: Las Posadas
www.littlepassports.com/blog/world-holidays/mexican-christmas-tradition/
Discover more about Las Posadas and learn how to make a holiday piñata!

Publisher's note to educators and parents: Our editors have carefully reviewed these websites to ensure that they are suitable for students. Many websites change frequently, however, and we cannot guarantee that a site's future contents will continue to meet our high standards of quality and educational value. Be advised that students should be closely supervised whenever they access the internet.

INDEX

Ecuador, 12
families, 4, 12, 14
food, 12, 20
Jesus Christ, 4, 6, 10, 11, 16, 22
Las Posadas, 6, 7
nativity scenes, 10, 11

Nochebuena, 10, 12
piñatas, 8, 9
Puerto Rico, 12, 14, 18
Three Wise Men, 16, 18, 19
traditions, 4, 22